Coton de Tulear

Coton de Tulear Dog Owner's Guide

Characteristics, Personality and Temperament, Diet, Health, Where to Buy, Cost, Rescue and Adoption, Care and Grooming, Training, Breeding, and Much More Included!

By Lolly Brown

Copyrights and Trademarks

All rights reserved. No part of this book may be reproduced or transformed in any form or by any means, graphic, electronic, or mechanical, including photocopying, recording, taping, or by any information storage retrieval system, without the written permission of the author.

This publication is Copyright ©2016. Nevada. All products, graphics, publications, software and services mentioned and recommended in this publication are protected by trademarks. In such instance, all trademarks & copyright belong to the respective owners. For information consult www.NRBpublishing.com

Disclaimer and Legal Notice

This product is not legal, medical, or accounting advice and should not be interpreted in that manner. You need to do your own due-diligence to determine if the content of this product is right for you. While every attempt has been made to verify the information shared in this publication, neither the author, neither publisher, nor the affiliates assume any responsibility for errors, omissions or contrary interpretation of the subject matter herein. Any perceived slights to any specific person(s) or organization(s) are purely unintentional.

We have no control over the nature, content and availability of the web sites listed in this book. The inclusion of any web site links does not necessarily imply a recommendation or endorse the views expressed within them. We take no responsibility for, and will not be liable for, the websites being temporarily unavailable or being removed from the internet.

The accuracy and completeness of information provided herein and opinions stated herein are not guaranteed or warranted to produce any particular results, and the advice and strategies, contained herein may not be suitable for every individual. Neither the author nor the publisher shall be liable for any loss incurred as a consequence of the use and application, directly or indirectly, of any information presented in this work. This publication is designed to provide information in regard to the subject matter covered.

Neither the author nor the publisher assume any responsibility for any errors or omissions, nor do they represent or warrant that the ideas, information, actions, plans, suggestions contained in this book is in all cases accurate. It is the reader's responsibility to find advice before putting anything written in this book into practice. The information in this book is not intended to serve as legal, medical, or accounting advice.

Foreword

The Coton de Tulear is a rare breed that boasts of a unique and beautiful cotton-like coat. The breed is only starting to gain popularity and has only been recently acknowledged by the American Kennel Club. These dogs are so irresistibly lovable with round eyes and an expressive smile that could melt your heart. Their wit and intelligence will surely bring loads of joy into your home.

If you're interested to bring home a Coton de Tulear, it would be wise to learn as much as you can about the breed so you can make an informed decision on whether you are capable of taking care of one. This book will help you become the best dog owner to a Coton de Tulear if you decide to get one. So turn the page and let the education begin!

Table of Contents

Introduction 1

   Glossary of Dog Terms 3

Chapter One: Understanding Coton de Tulears 1

   Facts About Coton de Tulears 2

      Summary of Coton de Tulears Facts 4

   Coton de Tulear Breed History 5

Chapter Two: Things to Know Before Getting a Coton de Tulear 7

   Do You Need a License? 8

   Do Coton de Tulears Get Along with Other Pets? 9

   How Many Coton de Tulears Should You Keep? 9

   How Much Does it Cost to Keep a Coton de Tulear? 10

      Initial Costs 10

      Monthly Costs 15

   What are the Pros and Cons of Coton de Tulear? 17

Chapter Three: Purchasing Coton de Tulears 19

   Where Can You Buy Coton de Tulears? 20

   Purchasing vs. Adopting a Rescue 22

   How to Choose a Reputable Coton de Tulear Breeder 25

   Tips for Selecting a Healthy Coton de Tulear Puppy 28

   Puppy-Proofing Your Home 31

Chapter Four: Caring for Coton de Tulears 35

    Before bringing your Coton de Tulear home 36

    Habitat and Exercise Requirements for Coton de Tulears 37

    Setting Up Your Puppy's Area 40

Chapter Five: Meeting Your Coton de Tulear's Nutritional Needs 43

    The Nutritional Needs of Coton de Tulear 44

    How to Select a High-Quality Dog Food Brand 45

    Tips for Feeding Your Coton de Tulear 48

    Dangerous Foods to Avoid 49

Chapter Six: Training Your Coton de Tulear 51

    Socializing Your New Coton de Tulear Puppy 52

    Positive Reinforcement for Obedience Training 54

    Negative Consequences for Respect Training 55

    Crate Training - Housebreaking Your Puppy 57

    Teaching Tricks and Playing Games 59

Chapter Seven: Grooming Your Coton de Tulear Properly . 63

    Recommended Tools to Have on Hand 64

    Recommended Brands for Grooming Supplies 65

    Tips for Bathing and Grooming Coton de Tulear 67

    Other Grooming Tasks 69

Chapter Eight: Breeding Coton de Tulears 71

Basic Dog Breeding Information 72

Breeding Tips and Raising Puppies 74

Chapter Nine: Showing Your Coton de Tulear 79

Coton de Tulear Breed Standard 80

Preparing Your Coton de Tulear for Show 84

Chapter Ten: Keeping Your Dog Healthy 87

Common Health Problems Affecting Coton de Tulears ... 88

Preventing Illness with Vaccinations 92

Coton de Tulear Care Sheet 95

1.) Basic Coton de Tulear Information 96

2.) Habitat Requirements 97

3.) Nutritional Needs 98

4.) Breeding Information 99

5.) First Aid Kit 100

Index 103

References 109

Photo Credits 111

Introduction

Bringing a dog home is a big responsibility and that responsibility begins when you're choosing the right breed for you. Choosing the right breed is like choosing a life partner because you're making a commitment and compatibility plays a big role. It's even more literal for dogs because they are the most loyal creatures in the world and they will live their entire lives as your companion. Isn't it a shame that they have shorter life spans than humans? So make the right choice because they deserve a good home where they will be loved and happy.

Introduction

This book is all about Coton de Tulears and basically contains all the important things you need to know when considering bringing one home as a pet.

The Coton de Tulear is a rare breed and not widely known. This breed is like a hidden treasure and those who discover it and decide to keep them as pets are rewarded with priceless wealth of happiness. Their distinct cotton coat makes them very beautiful. If you're looking for a companion, you can't go wrong with this breed because they are very loving and affectionate. Also, they are very intelligent and witty and are sure to keep you entertained. These are just a few of the lovable things about this breed.

But before even considering purchasing a Coton de Tulear, it would be smart to educate yourself first on what it really takes to be a dog owner and, specifically, to own a Coton de Tulear. To learn more about this wonderful breed and what it entails to keep one as a pet, please do read on.

Introduction

Glossary of Dog Terms

AKC – American Kennel Club, the largest purebred dog registry in the United States

Breed – A domestic race of dogs having a common gene pool and characterized appearance/function

Breed Standard – A published document describing the look, movement, and behavior of the perfect specimen of a particular breed

Coat – The hair covering of a dog; some breeds have two coats, and outer coat and undercoat; also known as a double coat. Examples of breeds with double coats include German Shepherd, Siberian Husky, Akita, etc.

Condition – The health of the dog as shown by its skin, coat, behavior, and general appearance

Crate – A container used to house and transport dogs; also called a cage or kennel

Groom – To brush, trim, comb or otherwise make a dog's coat neat in appearance

Kennel – A building or enclosure where dogs are kept

Litter – A group of puppies born at one time

Mate – To breed a male and female dog

Introduction

Neuter – To castrate a male dog or spay a female dog

Pedigree – The written record of a dog's genealogy going back three generations or more

Puppy – A dog under 12 months of age

Purebred – A dog whose sire and dam belong to the same breed and who are of unmixed descent

Shedding – The natural process whereby old hair falls off the dog's body as it is replaced by new hair growth.

Smooth Coat – Short hair that is close-lying

Spay – The surgery to remove a female dog's ovaries, rendering her incapable of breeding

Styptic powder – Remedy to stop bleeding

Trim – To groom a dog's coat by plucking or clipping

Wean – The process through which puppies transition from subsisting on their mother's milk to eating solid food

Whelping – The act of birthing a litter of puppies

Chapter One: Understanding Coton de Tulears

Coton de Tulears are easy to have as pets compared to other breeds and anyone would fall in love with their joyful and amiable personality. Indeed, their charm is irresistible. If you're entertaining the idea of getting a dog and you're looking for the perfect breed for you, the Coton de Tulear just might be the one. Start reading and learning about these precious gems to find out if you'll want to take one home. In this chapter you will find an overview of the Coton de Tulear including their history, physical characteristics and more.

Chapter One: Understanding Coton de Tulears

Facts About Coton de Tulears

If you're looking for the perfect breed of dog, the Coton de Tular comes very close to it. The drawbacks of owning the breed is greatly outnumbered by the benefits, and the drawbacks are tolerable and manageable. Caring for them as pets doesn't involve much fuss and problematic concerns. Their main characteristic is being a companion dog and they are everything that the word entails. They are a joy to have in your home with their clever tricks and huge presence despite their tiny size. Loving them will come naturally because of their pleasing personality and temperament. Coton de Tulears are highly intelligent, playful and energetic, sweet and affectionate, adaptable and easygoing. Side effects of these traits are charming, adorable, irresistible, endearing and all other synonyms.

In terms of size, their height ranges from 9 – 12 inches and the average weight for the breed is between 8 – 13 pounds. Their most distinct feature is their white cotton coat for which they are named after. They look like Maltese and Bichon due to distant ancestry relations. These breeds all share the same high-maintenance grooming of their coats.

Like all dogs and not unlike humans, Coton de Tulear dogs have unique personalities and different speeds in learning. They are generally very easy to train because of their intellect, though this exceptional brilliance may also

Chapter One: Understanding Coton de Tulears

prove to cause difficulties in behavior management which will be explained in its own section.

Aside from grooming concerns, another drawback of the breed is their potential for excessive barking. They tend to bark over anything that catches their interest or use it as a way to get your attention. These dogs are very needy of attention and they require frequent contact with their human. If left alone too often and too much, they become too noisy and may develop destructive behaviors to release their frustration. It would be good to know and understand that this breed may suffer from separation anxiety so if you can't commit to being around him for long periods of time, don't get one.

Their lifespan usually ranges between 14 – 19 years thanks to a healthy gene pool.

Chapter One: Understanding Coton de Tulears

Summary of Coton de Tulears Facts

Pedigree: Madagascar

AKC Group: Companion, Non-sporting

Breed Size: small and sturdy

Height: female dogs – 9 to 10 inches, male dogs – 10 to 11 inches

Weight: female dogs – 8 to 13 pounds, male dogs – 9 to 15 pounds

Coat Length: long

Coat Texture: cotton-like

Shedding: none

Color: white, occasional light tan or gray in ears

Eyes: brown or black

Nose: black

Ears: droopy

Tail: curved over the back

Temperament: affectionate, playful, adaptable, sociable, intelligent, easygoing

Strangers: generally friendly to everyone

Chapter One: Understanding Coton de Tulears

Children: generally good with children, but (like all dogs) should be supervised around young and small children

Other Dogs: generally good with other dogs and other animals if properly trained and socialized

Training: very easy

Exercise Needs: minimal exercise needed – daily walks, outdoor and indoor physical activities would be sufficient

Health Conditions: ordinarily no known health issues

Lifespan: 14 – 19 years

Coton de Tulear Breed History

Chapter One: Understanding Coton de Tulears

The Coton de Tulear is a rare and ancient breed. As expected of ancient breeds, their histories get muddled over time and a lot of the tales about the breed is unsubstantiated.

It is said that the Coton de Tulear originated at the port of Tulear in Madagascar when a pirate shipwreck brought its ancestor (potentially related to the Bichon) and it mated with a local dog that produced the lovely breed that is known now. They are known as the "Royal Dog of Madagascar" because before it was illegal for commoners to own one and only the royal courts or the elite were allowed. There are no details about its revival from extinction but in 1992 the government of Madagascar stopped the export of the dogs to prevent it.

Chapter Two: Things to Know Before Getting a Coton de Tulear

Now that you're acquainted with the Coton de Tulear, you should more or less already know whether the breed is right for you or not. However, before you decide to get one, you should take the time to learn about the practical aspects of owning a dog. It's not all fun and cuddles: owning dogs cost a lot. In this chapter you will find out just how much damage they can do to your bank account plus other practical material you need to know before embarking on the journey of being a dog owner. This chapter should help you further in making an educated decision on whether you are capable and ready to own a pet.

Chapter Two: Things to Know About Coton de Tulears

Do You Need a License?

Before purchasing a Coton de Tulear, you should learn about local licensing requirements that may affect you. The licensing requirements for dog owners vary from one country to another so you may need to do a little bit of research on your own to determine whether you need a dog license or not. In the United States, there are no federal requirements for dog licensing – it is determined at the state level. While some states do not, most states require dog owners to license their dogs on an annual basis.

When you apply for a dog license you will have to submit proof that your dog has been given a rabies vaccine. Dog licenses in the United States cost about $25 (£16.25) per year and they can be renewed annually when you renew your dog's rabies vaccine. Even if your state doesn't require you to license your dog it is still a good idea because it will help someone to identify him if he gets lost so they can return him to you.

In the United Kingdom, licensing requirements for dog owners are a little bit different. The U.K. requires that all dog owners license their dogs and the license can be renewed every twelve months. The cost to license your dog in the U.K. is similar to the U.S. but you do not have to have your dog vaccinated against rabies. In fact, rabies does not exist in the U.K. because it was eradicated through careful

Chapter Two: Things to Know About Coton de Tulears

control measures. If you travel with your dog to or from the U.K., you will have to obtain a special animal moving license and your dog may have to undergo a period of quarantine to make sure he doesn't carry disease into the country.

Do Coton de Tulears Get Along with Other Pets?

All breeds of dogs first need proper socialization in order to cultivate the potential for friendliness and companionability. Properly socialized Coton de Tulears generally enjoy the company of other pets especially when their humans are not around.

How Many Coton de Tulears Should You Keep?

There is no exact answer to this question because it depends on you. Coton de Tulears usually get along well with their fellow breed but each of them loves being the center of attention. So as long as you give them equal attention, you should be able to maintain a harmonious relationship among all of you. You can keep as much of them as you are capable of handling in all aspects – physically, mentally, emotionally, and financially.

Chapter Two: Things to Know About Coton de Tulears
How Much Does it Cost to Keep a Coton de Tulear?

Most people who aspire to own a dog don't realize that the cost is more than just the purchase price itself. Owning pets mean including them in your budget because the expenses are as a regular as your grocery and utility bills. Spending on your Coton de Tulear will begin even before you take him home because you have to prepare for his arrival and you have to purchase a crate, toys, indoor gates or fences, and food bowls. The responsibility of being a dog owner also includes being able to provide for their needs so before you take one home make sure that you can keep up with the expenses. In this section you will receive an overview of the initial costs and monthly costs to keep a Coton de Tulear.

Initial Costs

The initial costs for keeping a Coton de Tulear include those costs that you must cover before you can bring your dog home. Some of the initial costs you will need to cover include your dog's crate, food/water bowls, toys and accessories, microchipping, initial vaccinations, spay/neuter surgery and supplies for grooming and nail clipping – it also includes the cost of the dog itself.

Chapter Two: Things to Know About Coton de Tulears

You will find an overview of each of these costs as well as an estimate for each cost below:

Purchase Price–The cost to purchase a Coton de Tulear can vary greatly depending where you find the dog. You can adopt a rescue Coton de Tulear for as little as $250-$500 (£225-£450) but purchasing a puppy, especially a purebred puppy from an AKC-registered breeder, would be much more costly. The cost for a Coton de Tulear ranges from $1,800-$4,000 (£1,620-£3600). Just be cautious when buying from unregistered breeders and do a background check on their credibility. Make sure the puppy is completely healthy.

Crate–The Coton de Tulear is generally a small breed and will stay that way even if he's an adult already so you'll be able to save money that would otherwise be needed to buy a bigger one. The average cost for a small dog crate is about $30 (£19.50) in most cases.

Indoor Fences/Gates – Aside from the crate, you'll need to create a space for your puppy that he can acknowledge as his own where you will set up his bed and toys. The average cost for these fences/gates is $100 (£70).

Chapter Two: Things to Know About Coton de Tulears

Bed–It is ideal to teach your puppy early on that there is a designated place for him to sleep. An average bed costs $42 (£38).

Food/Water Bowls – In addition to providing your dog with a crate to sleep in, you should also make sure he has a set of high-quality food and water bowls. The best materials for these are stainless steel because it is easy to clean and doesn't harbor bacteria. Choose bowls that are heavy so that the dog won't be able to push or tip it over and make a mess. The average cost for a quality set of stainless steel bowls is about $20 (£18).

Toys – Giving your Coton de Tulears plenty of toys to play with will help to keep him from chewing on things that are not toys – they can also be used to provide mental stimulation and enrichment. To start out, plan to buy an assortment of toys for your dog until you learn what kind he prefers. You may want to budget a cost of $50 (£45) for toys just to be sure you have enough to last through the puppy phase. Coton de Tulears are fond of squeaky toys so you might want to keep that in mind.

Microchipping – In the United States and United Kingdom there are no federal or state requirements saying that you

Chapter Two: Things to Know About Coton de Tulears

have to have your dog microchipped, but it is a very good idea. Your dog could slip out of his collar on a walk or lose his ID tag. If someone finds him without identification, they can take him to a shelter to have his microchip scanned. A microchip is something that is implanted under your dog's skin and it carries a number that is linked to your contact information. The procedure takes just a few minutes to perform and it only costs about $30 (£19.50) in most cases.

Initial Vaccinations – During your dog's first year of life, he will require a number of different vaccinations. If you purchase your puppy from a reputable breeder, he might already have had a few but you'll still need more over the next few months as well as booster shots each year. You should budget about $50 (£32.50) for initial vaccinations just to be prepared.

Spay/Neuter Surgery – If you don't plan to breed your bulldog you should have him or her neutered or spayed before 6 months of age. The cost for this surgery will vary depending where you go and on the sex of your dog. If you go to a traditional veterinary surgeon, the cost for spay/neuter surgery could be very high but you can save money by going to a veterinary clinic. The average cost for neuter surgery is $50 to $100 (£32.50 - £65) and spay surgery costs about $100 to $200 (£65 - £130).

Chapter Two: Things to Know About Coton de Tulears

Supplies/Accessories – In addition to purchasing your bulldog's crate and food/water bowls, you should also purchase some basic grooming supplies as well as a leash and collar. The cost for these items will vary depending on the quality, but you should budget about $100 (£32.50) for these extra costs

Initial Costs for Coton de Tulears		
Cost	**One Dog**	**Two Dogs**
Purchase Price	$1,800-$4,000 (£1,620-£3,600)	$3600 - $8,000 (£3,240 - £7,200)
Crate	$30 (£19.50)	$60 (£39)
Fences/Gates	$100 (£70)	$100 (£70)
Bed	$42 (£38)	$84 (£76)
Food/Water Bowl	$20 (£18)	$40 (£36)
Toys	$50 (£45)	$100 (£90)
Microchipping	$30 (£19.50)	$60 (£39)
Vaccinations	$50 (£32.50)	$100 (£65)
Spay/Neuter	$50 to $200 (£32.50 - £130)	$100 to $400 (£65 - £260)
Accessories	$100 (£90)	$100 (£90)
Total	$602 to $2,672 (£542 - £2,405)	$1,094 to $5144 (£945 – £4,630)

Chapter Two: Things to Know About Coton de Tulears

*Costs may vary depending on location
**U.K. prices based on an estimated exchange of $1 = £0.90

Monthly Costs

The monthly costs for keeping a Coton de Tulear as a pet include those costs which recur on a monthly basis. The most important monthly cost for keeping a dog is, of course, food. In addition to food, however, you'll also need to think about things like annual license renewal, toy replacements, and veterinary exams. <u>You will find an overview of each of these costs as well as an estimate for each cost on below</u>:

Food and Treats – Feeding your Coton de Tulear a healthy diet is very important for his health and wellness. A high-quality diet for dogs is not cheap, so you should be prepared to spend around $35 (£31.50) on a large bag of high-quality dog food which will last you at least a month. You should also include a monthly budget of about $10 (£6.50) for treats.

Grooming Costs – The Coton de Tulear's cottony coat will require professional grooming. Certain cuts and trims will make your dog's coat easier to maintain but a show-quality coat will need frequent brushing and grooming. You should plan a budget for the cost of professional grooming four

Chapter Two: Things to Know About Coton de Tulears

times per year. The average cost for a professional grooming visit is between $50 and $75 (£32.50 – £68). This divided into 4 visits per year, equals a monthly grooming cost around $17 to $25 (£15 - £22.50).

License Renewal – The cost to license your Coton de Tulear will generally be about $25 (£16.25) and you can renew the license for the same price each year. License renewal cost divided over 12 months is about $2 (£1.30) per month.

Veterinary Exams – In order to keep your Coton de Tulear healthy you should take him to the veterinarian about every six months after he passes puppyhood. You might have to take him more often for the first 12 months to make sure he gets his vaccines on time. The average cost for a vet visit is about $40 (£26) so, if you have two visits per year, it averages to about $7 (£4.55) per month. However, depending on how healthy or unhealthy your dog is, this amount is relative to the medical care he will need.

Other Costs – In addition to the monthly costs for your bulldog's food, license renewal, and vet visits there are also some other cost you might have to pay occasionally. These costs might include things like replacements for worn-out toys, a larger collar as your puppy grows, cleaning products,

Chapter Two: Things to Know About Coton de Tulears

and more. You should budget about $15 (£9.75) per month for extra costs.

Monthly Costs for Coton de Tulears		
Cost	One Dog	Two Dogs
Food and Treats	$45 (£40.50)	$90 (£81)
Grooming Costs	$17 to $25 (£15 - £22.50)	$34 to $50 (£31 - £45)
License Renewal	$2 (£1.30)	$4 (£3.60)
Veterinary Exams	$7 (£4.55)	$14 (£12.60)
Other Costs	$15 (£9.75)	$30 (£19.50)
Total	$86 to $94 (£78 – £85)	$172 to $188 (£155 - £169)

*Costs may vary depending on location
**U.K. prices based on an estimated exchange of $1 = £0.90

What are the Pros and Cons of Coton de Tulear?

With an overall adorable personality and appearance, these dogs are tantalizingly endearing. So if you're one of those people who has fallen for the charm of the Coton de Tulear, it would be wise to get to know more about having them as a pet and the best way to help you decide is to learn the good and the bad about them. You will find a list of pros and cons for the Coton de Tulear breed below:

Chapter Two: Things to Know About Coton de Tulears

Pros for the Coton de Tulear Breed

- Adaptable, laid back, companionable, affectionate, brainy
- Easy to train
- Minimal exercise requirement
- Very sociable to people and animals
- No health concerns
- No shedding
- Hypoallergenic dogs so they are good for people with allergies or sensitive skin

Cons for the Coton de Tulear Breed

- Expensive purchase price
- Prone to excessive barking
- Clingy dogs that suffer from separation anxiety and may become destructive when left alone too much (not suitable for people who are away from home often)
- Hard to groom

Chapter Three: Purchasing Coton de Tulears

Getting a dog is a process that requires a lot of thinking, weighing options and researching for the right place to get your dog. It's also very exciting because you are faced with the prospect of meeting the newest addition to your home. In this chapter you will find out where you can get your dog and you will read about the advantages and disadvantages of purchasing versus adopting a Coton de Tulear. Once you've weighed your options, you can refer to the guides in choosing a breeder, selecting a healthy puppy, and puppy-proofing your home.

Chapter Three: Purchasing Coton de Tulears

Where Can You Buy Coton de Tulears?

When you've made a decision to become a dog owner, the fun begins as soon as you start hunting for the dog that will win your heart and make you want to take him home.

Many people think that the best place to find a dog is at the pet store but, unfortunately, they are greatly mistaken. While the puppies at the pet store might look cute and cuddly, there is no way to know whether they are actually healthy or well-bred. Many pet stores get their puppies from puppy mills and they sell the puppies to unsuspecting dog lovers. Puppy mill puppies are often already sick by the time they make it to the pet store, often traveling across state lines to get there.

A puppy mill is a type of breeding facility that focuses on breeding and profit more than the health and wellbeing of the dogs. Puppy mills usually keep their dogs in squalid conditions, forcing them to bear litter after litter of puppies with little to no rest in between. Many of the breeders used in puppy mills are poorly bred themselves or unhealthy to begin with which just ensures that the puppies will have the same problems. The only time you should bring home a puppy from a pet store is if the store has a partnership with a local shelter and that is where they get

Chapter Three: Purchasing Coton de Tulears

their dogs. If the pet store can't tell you which breeder the puppies came from, or if they don't offer you any paperwork or registration for the puppy, it is likely that the puppy came from a puppy mill.

Rather than purchasing a puppy from a pet store, your best bet is to find a reputable Coton de Tulear breeder – preferably and AKC-registered breeder in the United States or a Kennel Club-registered breeder in the U.K. If you visit the website for either of these organizations you can find a list of breeders for all of the club-recognized breeds. You can also look for breeders on the website for other breed clubs like the United States of America Coton de Tulear Club and the Madagascar Coton de Tulear Club of America or Coton de Tuléar in the United Kingdom. Even if these organizations don't provide a list of breeders you may be able to speak with members to find out more.

Chapter Three: Purchasing Coton de Tulears

Purchasing vs. Adopting a Rescue

If you don't have your heart set on a puppy, you may consider adopting a rescue from a local shelter. A common misconception about rescue dogs is that there is something wrong with them but in the case of this breed, they are usually healthy and well-trained and they only end up in the shelter because they either got lost or their owners are no longer capable of taking care of them. Sometimes backyard breeders aren't able to sell the whole litter and the ones that remain are sent to the shelter. There are many benefits associated with rescuing an adult Coton de Tulear. While there is only one disadvantage: it is quite difficult to find a Coton de Tulear in shelters because they are a rare breed and you may have to wait for the availability of one or if you don't want to wait you might have to go farther than your

Chapter Three: Purchasing Coton de Tulears

current location to find one. One benefit of adopting is that adoption fees are generally $500 (£450) or less which is much more affordable than the $1,800 to $4,000 (£1,620-£3600) fee to buy a puppy from a breeder. Plus, an adult dog will already be housetrained. Rescue groups take very good care of these dogs and make sure they are well-trained and good-mannered and healthy. As an added bonus, most shelters spay/neuter their dogs before adopting them out so you won't have to pay for the surgery yourself. Another benefit is that an adult dog has already surpassed the puppy stage so his personality is set – with a puppy you can never quite be sure how your puppy will turn out. If you choose to adopt a Coton de Tulear, you are doing a very honorable thing because you are giving a home to the homeless. These dogs also deserve a home and someone who will love them. You might even be saving a life because every year approximately 4 million adoptable animals are killed and surely at least one of them is a Coton de Tulear.

If you are considering adopting a Coton de Tulear, consider one of these breed-specific rescues:

United States Rescues:

UCARE
<http://cotonrescue.us/>

Chapter Three: Purchasing Coton de Tulears

American Coton Club Foster & Adoption
<http://www.americancotonclub.com/rescue.htm>

Adopt a Coton de Tulear
<http://www.adoptapet.com/s/adopt-a-coton-de-tulear>

United Coton de Tulear Association for Rescue and Education
<http://awos.petfinder.com/shelters/cotonrescue.html>

The Rescue of the Coton de Tulear
<http://www.furbabyrescue.com/Coton.html>

United Kingdom Rescues:

Coton de Tulear Breed Rescue
<http://www.thekennelclub.org.uk/services/public/findarescue/Default.aspx?breed=6252>

Coton de Tulear Re-homing Group
<http://www.cdtclubuk.org/#/re-homing/4563148764>

Chapter Three: Purchasing Coton de Tulears

How to Choose a Reputable Coton de Tulear Breeder

When you are ready to start looking for Coton de Tulear puppy, you may begin your search for a breeder online. A simple internet search will probably give you a variety of results but, if you want to find a reputable breeder, you may have to dig a little deeper. United States of America Coton de Tulear Club and the Madagascar Coton de Tulear Club of America or Coton de Tuléar in the United Kingdom are great places to start. Compile a list of breeders from whatever sources you can and then take the time to go through each option to determine whether the breeder is reputable and responsible or not. You do not want to run the risk of purchasing a puppy from a hobby breeder or from someone who doesn't follow responsible breeding practices. If you aren't careful about where you get your puppy, you could end up with a puppy that is already sick.

Once you have your list of breeders on hand you can go through them one-by-one to narrow down your options. Go through the following steps to do so:

- Visit the website for each breeder on your list (if they have one) and look for key points about the breeder's history and experience.
    - Check for club registrations and a license, if applicable.

- - If the website doesn't provide any information about the facilities or the breeder you are best just moving on.
- After ruling out some of the breeders, contact the remaining breeders on your list by phone
  - Ask the breeder the following questions:
    - How old are the parents?
    - Can you provide me with the health clearances of the parents?
    - Why did you decide upon this particular breeding?
    - Can you tell me about the dogs in the 3 generation pedigree?
    - How did you raise the puppies? Have you started training and socializing?
    - Can you provide references from previous buyers?
  - The answers to these questions must be along these lines:
    - The female dog must not be younger than 18 months and the male should not be younger than 12 months. Dogs must be given time to mature before being bred.
    - The breeder must be able to present you with a Canine Health Information Center number as an assurance that the

Chapter Three: Purchasing Coton de Tulears

- parents were screened and deemed healthy and fit to be bred.
  - The answer should have been well-thought out and it should include a rational objective.
  - A good breeder will be able to give you a detailed account of the 3 generation pedigree without batting an eyelash because he knows it by heart and he is proud of it.
  - The breeder should have already started introducing the world to the puppy and should be able to teach you how to continue training and socialization.
  - A good breeder stays in touch with the owners to provide assistance so he should be able to give you references.
  - Expect a reputable breeder to ask you questions about yourself as well – a responsible breeder wants to make sure that his puppies go to good homes.
- Schedule an appointment to visit the facilities for the remaining breeders on your list after you've weeded a few more of them out.
  - Ask for a tour of the facilities, including the place where the breeding stock is kept as well as the facilities housing the puppies.

Chapter Three: Purchasing Coton de Tulears

- o If things look unorganized or unclean, do not purchase from the breeder.
- o Make sure the breeding stock is in good condition and that the puppies are all healthy-looking and active.
- Narrow down your list to a final few options and then interact with the puppies to make your decision.
  - o Make sure the breeder provides some kind of health guarantee and ask about any vaccinations the puppies may have already received.
- Put down a deposit, if needed, to reserve a puppy if they aren't ready to come home yet.

Tips for Selecting a Healthy Coton de Tulear Puppy

Chapter Three: Purchasing Coton de Tulears

After you have narrowed down your options for breeders you then need to pick out your puppy. If you are a first-time dog owner, do not let yourself become caught up in the excitement of a new puppy – take the time to make a careful selection. If you rush the process you could end up with a puppy that isn't healthy or one whose personality isn't compatible with your family. <u>Follow the steps below to pick out your Coton de Tulear puppy</u>:

- Ask the breeder to give you a tour of the facilities, especially where the puppies are kept.
    - Make sure the facilities where the puppies are housed are clean and sanitary – if there is evidence of diarrhea, do not purchase one of the puppies because they may already be sick.
- Take a few minutes to observe the litter as a whole, watching how the puppies interact with each other.
    - The puppies should be active and playful, interacting with each other in a healthy way.
    - Avoid puppies that appear to be lethargic and those that have difficulty moving – they are most probably sick.
- Approach the litter and watch how the puppies react to you when you do.
    - If the puppies appear frightened they may not be properly socialized and you do not want a puppy like that.

Chapter Three: Purchasing Coton de Tulears

- o Some of the puppies may be somewhat cautious, but most of them should be very friendly, curious and interested in you.
- Let the puppies approach you and give them time to sniff and explore you before you interact with them.
  - o Pet the puppies and encourage them to play with a toy, taking the opportunity to observe their personalities.
  - o Single out any of the puppies that you think might be a good fit and spend a little time with them.
- Pick up the puppy and hold him to see how he responds to human contact.
  - o The puppy should be affectionate and playful. It shouldn't be frightened of you and it should enjoy being pet.
- Examine the puppy's body for signs of illness and injury
  - o The puppy should have clear, bright eyes with no discharge. The coat should be even, no patches of hair loss or discoloration.
  - o The ears should be bat ears, clean and clear with no discharge or inflammation.
  - o The nose should be black. The only time lighter colored noses are acceptable is if the dog's color is lighter as well.

Chapter Three: Purchasing Coton de Tulears

- o The puppy's stomach may be round but it shouldn't be distended or swollen.
- o The puppy should be able to walk and run normally without any mobility problems.
- If you're entertaining the idea of participating in dog shows, you should learn about the disqualifications of the breed standard (which can be found in Chapter 9 of this book) so you know which qualities to watch out for and refrain from buying.
- Narrow down your options and choose the puppy that you think is the best fit.

Once you've chosen your puppy, ask the breeder about the next steps. Do not take the puppy home if it isn't at least 8 weeks old and unless it has been fully weaned and is already eating solid food.

Puppy-Proofing Your Home

After you've picked out your puppy you may still have to wait a few weeks until you can bring him home. During this time you should take steps to prepare your home, making it a safe place for your puppy. The process of making your home safe for your puppy is called "puppy proofing" and it involves removing or storing away anything and everything that could harm your puppy. It

Chapter Three: Purchasing Coton de Tulears

might help for you to crawl around the house on your hands and knees, viewing things from your puppy's perspective to find potential threats.

<u>On the following page you will find a list of things you should do when you are puppy-proofing your home:</u>

- Make sure your trash and recycling containers have a tight-fitting lid or store them in a cabinet.

- Put away all open food containers and keep them out of reach of your puppy.

- Store cleaning products and other hazardous chemicals in a locked cabinet or pantry where your puppy can't get them.

- Make sure electrical cords and blind pulls are wrapped up and placed out of your puppy's reach.

- Pick up any small objects or toys that could be a choking hazard if your puppy chews on them.

- Cover or drain any open bodies of water such as the toilet, and outdoor pond, etc.

Chapter Three: Purchasing Coton de Tulears

- Store any medications and beauty products in the medicine cabinet out of your puppy's reach.

- Check your home for any plants that might be toxic to dogs and remove them or put them out of reach.

- Block off fire places, windows, and doors so your puppy can't get into trouble.

- Close off any stairwells and block the entry to rooms where you do not want your puppy to be.

Chapter Three: Purchasing Coton de Tulears

Chapter Four: Caring for Coton de Tulears

After learning about the practical aspects of keeping a Coton de Tulear as a pet, you can now move on to learning how to care for your dog and the tasks involved. It is important to create a loving and safe environment where your dog can feel at home and live his long, healthy life in harmony with you. This section talks about your dog's habitat and exercise requirements, and will teach you how to prepare your home and make it an ideal place for your puppy.

Chapter Four: Caring for Coton de Tulears

Before bringing your Coton de Tulear home

You should ask yourself these questions first:

- **Do you spend most of your time away from home? If yes, will you be able to bring your dog along with you?**
Coton de Tulears don't like being alone or away from their owners for long periods of time and they suffer from separation anxiety. It'll be cruel to subject them to that if you're just planning on leaving them at home all the time.
- **Will you be able to keep up with the grooming needs of your Coton de Tulear?**
Coton de Tulears are known to be high-maintenance in terms of grooming so you have to make sure you can provide the necessary care or pay for grooming services.
- **Do you have what it takes to be a firm, consistent, and patient trainer?**
These are all requirements for any well-behaved dog.
- **Can you tolerate excessive barking?**
This breed tends to bark a lot so you have to be able to tolerate the noise.

For families, it would also be a good idea to sit down and ask all members if they are all on board with getting a dog. Once the decision is agreed upon, you can all discuss

Chapter Four: Caring for Coton de Tulears

house rules and the distribution of tasks when caring for the dog (e.g. off-limits areas, feeding time, potty time, etc.) However, you should assign only one member of the family who will be the primary authority figure of the dog and will be in charge of housebreaking and training at all times.

Habitat and Exercise Requirements for Coton de Tulears

The Coton de Tulear is a very adaptable breed, but they are considered indoor companion dogs. Expect them to be your shadow around the house and to try to catch your attention by clowning around. They don't require big yards for daily exercise. A daily walk outside, or indoor games will be sufficient for his exercise needs. This breed is ordinarily

Chapter Four: Caring for Coton de Tulears

very friendly towards other dogs so it would be a good idea to get another dog as his companion as it will be the best way to ensure that he gets exercise because they will surely keep each other active inside or outside the house. Coton de Tulears are naturally playful and are born retrievers so they enjoy fetching and will never run out of energy to bring you back anything you throw. Despite their soft fur which makes them look a bit delicate, they are actually sturdy dogs who are fit for hiking and long walks. They are also attracted to water and love to play under the rain and go swimming.

Now, let's move on to how you can ensure that your dog feels at-home and is comfortable. First, you will need to provide him with certain things. A crate is one of the most important things you will need when you bring your new puppy home. Not only will it be a place for your puppy to sleep, but it will also be a place where you can confine him during the times when you are away from home or when you cannot keep a close eye on him. Your puppy will also need some other basic things like a water bowl, a food bowl, a collar, a leash, toys, and grooming supplies.

When shopping for food and water bowls, safety and sanitation are the top two considerations. Stainless steel is the best material to go with because it is easy to clean and resistant to bacteria. Ceramic is another good option. Heavy bowls are also a plus because the puppy will be unable to tip it over or push it across the floor which will save you from

Chapter Four: Caring for Coton de Tulears

cleaning unnecessary mess. Avoid plastic food and water bowls because they can become scratched and the scratches may harbor bacteria. You should choose a collar that is appropriate to his size. This may mean that you will purchase several collars and leashes while your puppy is still growing. A harness will be helpful during leash training because it will improve your control over your puppy.

Provide your puppy with an assortment of different toys and let him figure out which ones he likes. Having a variety of toys around the house is very important because you'll need to use them to redirect your puppy's natural chewing behavior as he learns what he is and is not allowed to chew on. As for grooming supplies, you'll need a wire-pin brush, metal wide-tooth comb, slicker brush (or undercoat rake) for daily brushing.

Above all, what you need to remember is that the Coton de Tulear will thrive in a home where there is an endless supply of human affection, attention and love.

Chapter Four: Caring for Coton de Tulears

Setting Up Your Puppy's Area

Before you bring your Coton de Tulear puppy home, you should set up a particular area in your home for him to call his own. The ideal setup will include your puppy's crate, a comfy dog bed, his food and water bowls, an assortment of toys, and litter trays since this breed are indoor dogs. You can arrange all of these items in a small room that is easy to block off using indoor fences or gates, or you can use a puppy playpen to give your puppy some free space while still keeping him somewhat confined. It would be ideal to choose a room where most of the activity in the house happens so that your puppy won't feel isolated.

Chapter Four: Caring for Coton de Tulears

When you bring your puppy home you'll have to work with him a lot to get him used to the crate. It is very important that you do this because the last thing you want is your puppy to form a negative association with the crate. If this happens, it will be very difficult to make your puppy forget it and it will most likely ruin your success at house training. It is vital that your puppy learns that the crate is his own special place, a place where he can go to relax and take a nap if he wants to. If you use the crate as punishment, your puppy will not want to use it.

To get your puppy used to the crate, try tossing a few treats into it and let him go fish them out. Feeding your puppy his meals in the crate with the door open will be helpful as well. You can also incorporate the crate into your playtime, tossing toys into the crate or hiding treats under a blanket in the crate. As your puppy gets used to the crate you can start keeping him in it with the door closed for short periods of time, working your way up to longer periods. Just be sure to let your puppy outside before and after you confine him and never force him to stay in the crate for longer than he is physically capable of holding his bowels and his bladder.

Chapter Four: Caring for Coton de Tulears

Chapter Five: Meeting Your Coton de Tulear's Nutritional Needs

As a dog owner, it is your duty to ensure that your dog lives a long and healthy life, and in order to do that you have to learn what and how to feed him. Like all living beings, dogs need proper nutrition and their needs are different from humans. So you'll have to take the time to learn the proper diet your dog needs. This chapter will tackle the nutritional needs of a Coton de Tulear and will help you in choosing high-quality dog food. You will also learn tips on feeding your puppy to ensure that you'll keep him healthy.

Chapter Five: Meeting Your Dog's Nutritional Needs

The Nutritional Needs of Coton de Tulear

Like all mammals, dogs require a balance of protein, carbohydrate and fat in their diets – this is in addition to essential vitamins and minerals. It is important to understand, however, that your dog's nutritional needs are very different from your own. For dogs, protein is the most important nutritional consideration followed by fat and then carbohydrates. In order to keep your dog healthy you need to create a diet that provides the optimal levels of these three macronutrients.

The portion of your dog's diet that comes from protein should be made up of animal sources like meat, poultry, and fish as well as meat meals. Protein is made up of amino acids which are the building blocks that make up your dog's tissues and cells. It also provides some energy for your dog. The most highly concentrated type of energy your Coton de Tulear needs, however, is fat. This nutrient is particularly important for small-breed dogs because they have very fast metabolisms and therefore very high needs for energy.

Consider this – small-breed dogs have higher needs for calories by bodyweight than large dogs. A large-breed dog like a 110-pound Akita, for example, might need a total daily calorie intake of 2,500 calories, but that only amounts

Chapter Five: Meeting Your Dog's Nutritional Needs

to about 23 calories per pound of bodyweight. An 8-pound Coton de Tulear, on the other hand, might only need 250 calories per day but that equates to about 45 calories per pound of its total bodyweight. A significant portion of these calories needs to come from fat in order to meet your dog's nutritional needs.

In addition to protein and fat, your dog also needs carbohydrates to provide dietary fiber and various vitamins and minerals. Dogs do not have a specific need for carbohydrates but they should always come from digestible sources since a dog's digestive tract is not designed to process plant foods as effectively as protein and fat. Your dog also needs plenty of fresh water on a daily basis as well as key vitamins and minerals.

How to Select a High-Quality Dog Food Brand

Shopping for dog food can be difficult for some dog owners simply because there are so many different options to choose from. If you walk into your local pet store you will see multiple aisles filled with bags of dog food from different brands and most brands offer a number of different formulas. So how do you choose a healthy dog food for your Coton de Tulear dog?

Chapter Five: Meeting Your Dog's Nutritional Needs

The best place to start when shopping for dog food is to read the dog food label. Pet food in the United States is loosely regulated by the American Association of Feed Control Officials (AAFCO) and they evaluate commercial dog food products according to their ability to meet the basic nutritional needs of dogs in various life stages. If the product meets these basic needs, the label will carry some kind of statement from AAFCO like this:

"[Product Name] is formulated to meet the nutritional levels established by the AAFCO Dog Food nutrient profiles for [Life Stage]."

If the dog food product you are looking at contains this statement you can move on to reading the ingredients list. Dog food labels are organized in descending order by volume. This means that the ingredients at the top of the list are used in higher quantities than the ingredients at the end of the list. This being the case, you want to see high-quality sources of animal protein at the beginning of the list. Things like fresh meat, poultry or fish are excellent ingredients but they contain about 80% water. After the product is cooked, the actual volume and protein content of the ingredient will be less. Meat meals (like chicken meal or salmon meal) have

Chapter Five: Meeting Your Dog's Nutritional Needs

already been cooked down so they contain up to 300% more protein by weight than fresh meats.

In addition to high-quality animal proteins, you want to check the ingredients list for digestible carbohydrates and healthy fats. For dogs, digestible carbohydrates include things like brown rice and oatmeal, as long as they have been cooked properly. You can also look for gluten-free and grain-free options like sweet potato and tapioca. It is best to avoid products that are made with corn, wheat, or soy ingredients because they are low in nutritional value and may trigger food allergies in your dog.

In terms of fat, you want to see at least one animal source such as chicken fat or salmon oil. Plant-based fats like flaxseed and canola oil are not necessarily bad, but they are less biologically valuable for your dog. If they are accompanied by an animal source of fat, it is okay. Just make sure that the fats included in the recipe provide a blend of both omega-3 and omega-6 fatty acids. This will help to preserve the quality and condition of your dog's skin and coat.

In addition to checking the ingredients list for beneficial ingredients you should also know that there are certainly things you do NOT want to see listed. Avoid products made with low-quality fillers like corn gluten meal or rice bran – you should also avoid artificial colors, flavors, and preservatives. Some commonly used artificial preservatives are BHA and BHT. In most cases the label will tell you if natural preservatives are used.

Tips for Feeding Your Coton de Tulear

Some dogs can be overly enthusiastic during mealtimes and they tend to eat too fast or too much so it would be a good idea to watch as he eats and make sure he doesn't gobble up his food too fast. The trick is to control the amount by giving him small portions, and then wait a while before giving again. This is important because eating rapidly may cause your dog's stomach to flip, which is a very serious and sometimes fatal medical condition known as Gastric dilation and volvulus. Another way to avoid this is by feeding your pet four times spread out through the day. That's the ideal method for feeding but if you don't have the time for it, twice or thrice a day should be fine as long as you implement the supervision technique discussed earlier.

Coton de Tulears need ¾ cup of high-quality dog food daily split according to his meal schedule.

Chapter Five: Meeting Your Dog's Nutritional Needs

Dangerous Foods to Avoid

It might be tempting to give in to your dog when he is begging at the table, but certain "people foods" can actually be toxic for your dog. As a general rule, you should never feed your dog anything unless you are 100% sure that it is safe. <u>Below you will find a list of foods that can be toxic to dogs and should therefore be avoided</u>:

- Alcohol
- Apple seeds
- Avocado
- Cherry pits
- Chocolate
- Coffee
- Garlic
- Grapes/raisins
- Hops
- Macadamia nuts
- Mold
- Mushrooms
- Mustard seeds
- Onions/leeks
- Peach pits
- Potato leaves/stems
- Rhubarb leaves
- Tea
- Tomato leaves/stems
- Walnuts
- Xylitol
- Yeast dough

If your dog eats any of these foods, contact the Pet Poison Control hotline right away at (888) 426 – 4435.

Chapter Five: Meeting Your Dog's Nutritional Needs

Chapter Six: Training Your Coton de Tulear

One of the joys of owning a Coton de Tulear is having a supremely smart dog that is easily trainable and eager to please. Obedience and respect training isn't as hard as it is with other dog breeds. But also be warned that because of their exceptional intelligence, they are capable of outsmarting you if you're too lenient on them. And if not properly trained, they can be quite mischievous and come up with clever ways to make trouble when left to their own devices. But you have to admit that dogs could pull off this trait as charming, endearing and funny all at the same time. Nonetheless, don't miss out on the fun of training this breed and turn the page to start learning all about it.

Chapter Six: Training Your Coton de Tulear

Socializing Your New Coton de Tulear Puppy

The first three months of life is when your puppy will be the most impressionable. This is when you need to socialize him because the experiences he has as a puppy will shape the way he interacts with the world as an adult. Coton de Tulears are usually very sociable and are known to be affectionate even to strangers, but without proper socialization, then they could grow up to be a mal-adjusted adult who fears new experiences, just like humans. Fortunately, socialization is very simple – all you have to do is make sure that your puppy has plenty of new experiences. <u>Below you will find a list of things you should expose your puppy to for properly socialization</u>:

- Introduce your puppy to friends in the comfort of your own home.

- Invite friends with dogs or puppies to come meet your puppy (make sure everyone is vaccinated).

- Expose your puppy to people of different sizes, shapes, gender, and skin color.

- Introduce your puppy to children of different ages – just make sure they know how to handle the puppy

Chapter Six: Training Your Coton de Tulear

safely.

- Take your puppy with you in the car when you run errands.

- Walk your puppy in as many places as possible so he is exposed to different surfaces and surroundings.

- Expose your puppy to water from hoses, sprinklers, showers, etc. Be sure to have control over your puppy when introducing him to bodies of water that could drown him.

- Make sure your puppy experiences loud noises such as fireworks, cars backfiring, loud music, thunder, etc.

- Introduce your puppy to various appliances and tools such as blenders, lawn mowers, vacuums, etc.

- Walk your puppy with different types of collars and leashes.

- Once he is old enough, take your puppy to the dog park to interact with other dogs.

Chapter Six: Training Your Coton de Tulear

Positive Reinforcement for Obedience Training

Training a dog is not as difficult as many people think – it all has to do with the rewards. Think about this – if you want someone to do something for you, you probably offer them something in return. The same concept is true for dog training – if you reward your dog for performing a particular behavior then he will be more likely to repeat it in the future. This is called positive reinforcement training and it is one of the simplest yet most effective training methods you can use as a dog owner.

The key to success with dog training is two-fold. For one thing, you need to make sure that your dog understands what it is you are asking him. If he doesn't know what a

Chapter Six: Training Your Coton de Tulear

command means it doesn't matter how many times you say it, he won't respond correctly. In order to teach your dog what a command means you should give it and then guide him to perform the behavior. Once he does, immediately give him a treat and praise him – the sooner you reward after identifying the desired behavior, the faster your puppy will learn.

The second key to success in dog training is consistency. While your puppy is learning basic obedience commands you need to use the same commands each and every time and you need to be consistent in rewarding him. If you maintain consistency it should only take a few repetitions for your puppy to learn what you expect of him. You can then move on to another command and alternate between them to reinforce your puppy's understanding.

Being people pleasers, Coton de Tulears respond best to this kind of training as they love to be showered with praises and rewards.

Negative Consequences for Respect Training

For a well-mannered dog who will not only follow you when you ask him to do something but who will also obey you when you ask him to stop doing unwanted actions, you need to earn his respect. Therefore, positive

Chapter Six: Training Your Coton de Tulear

reinforcement is not enough training because it doesn't teach your dog to respect you. When your dog is not in the mood for a treat, they will just opt not to listen to your command. Dogs have different personalities just like humans. The Coton de Tulear is usually obedient but of course there are still the occasional stubborn ones who need this kind of training more. Applicable to all dog breeds, you cannot ever let them think that you are their follower or else you will have problems in getting them to listen and obey you. Hence, respect training is a must. You have to establish rules so he'll know that you're capable of being his leader. When he misbehaves, you have to tell him "no" or "stop". You have to be firm but very gentle. Never hurt, scold or yell at your Coton de Tulear because and they don't respond to harshness. Respect training will probably be a bit harder than basic obedience training because of several reasons. The first reason is their high sensitivity level and how you must take extra care to be extremely conscious of your tone of voice, volume and gestures. The second reason is their extraordinary brilliance. As the saying goes, "too much of anything is bad," it proves to be correct in this case because these dogs use this aptitude to create naughty schemes. It makes respect training difficult because at first the frequency will be often and will lessen gradually as the training takes effect, which makes it all the more important to take the task seriously. The last reason would probably seem the most inconsequential but you might soon discover that it is the

Chapter Six: Training Your Coton de Tulear

most challenging of all: Coton de Tulears are just too irresistibly cute! And be warned that they will always try to use this to their advantage by turning on their full blast charm when they know they've done something wrong. It is essential to being their leader that you must not give in to them no matter how adorable those puppy eyes are. It will do you well to remember that their intellect makes them quick to learn both good and bad habits and if you don't curb the bad behaviors mentioned in the second and third reason, they will form as habits. If this happens, it means you have failed to earn their respect and their recognition of you as their master, which then makes you their follower. It is not the ideal situation to find yourself in so don't let it happen.

Crate Training - Housebreaking Your Puppy

In addition to obedience training, house training is very important for puppies. After all, you don't want to spend your dog's entire life following after him with a pooper scooper. Housebreaking a Coton de Tulear depends on the personality of your dog. Some of them are particularly slow to pick up on the routine, others learn just fine or quickly. You only have to be patient and consistent. The key to housebreaking is to use your puppy's crate appropriately. When you are able to watch your puppy, keep him in the same room with you at all times and point to the litter tray in his special area once every hour or so to give him a chance to do his business. Always lead him to the litter tray and give him a command like "Go pee" so he learns what is expected of him when you take him to this area. When he succeeds at this task, be sure to reward him.

When you can't watch your puppy and overnight, you should confine him to his crate. The crate should be just large enough for your puppy to stand up, sit down, turn around and lie down in. Keeping it this size will ensure that he views the crate as his den and he will be reluctant to soil it. Just make sure that you don't keep your puppy in the crate for longer than he is physically capable of holding his bladder. Always take your puppy out before putting him in the crate and immediately after releasing him.

If you give your puppy ample opportunity to do his business in his litter tray, reward him consistently, and you keep him confined to the crate when you can't watch him, housetraining should eventually be effective. Although, the length of training is also dependent on your dog's personality. Again, consistency and positive reinforcement – not to mention patience – is crucial here so always reward and praise your puppy for doing his business in his litter trays so he learns to do it that way. If your puppy does have an accident, do not punish him because not only will he not

Chapter Six: Training Your Coton de Tulear

understand – he won't associate the punishment with the crime so he will just learn to fear you instead – but also, as stated in the previous section, Coton de Tulear are highly sensitive to scolding or negative criticism.

Teaching Tricks and Playing Games

A worthwhile way of bonding and spending quality time with your Coton de Tulear is to incorporate play time with teaching tricks that is sure to be filled with a lot of fun and enjoyment for both of you. This is the most fun and easy part in training your Coton de Tulear because they are naturally adept at learning tricks. In fact, they prefer it more than obedience training. A common trait of this breed is their supernatural-like ability to understand what their owners want from them, sometimes even before a command is given. Moreover, they are able to understand multiple commands. Before you start teaching tricks, you have to remember that only positive reinforcement should be applied. When either of you start to get frustrated, just stop immediately. Never punish your dog for not being able to do the trick. <u>In the following page, you will learn how to teach certain tricks that are favored among the Coton de Tulear:</u>

Chapter Six: Training Your Coton de Tulear

Wave – Show your dog that you have a treat in your hand, close your fist, place it near him, then wait for him to paw at it. Once he paws at it, say "good wave". Give him the treat. Repeat several times. Then command him to sit down. Get another treat. Strategically place your fist just beyond his reach and he will look like he's waving. Keep repeating "good wave" each time so that he can eventually learn to do it with just the command and without the treat.

High five – Teach this trick after your dog masters the wave. When he waves, you place the pads of his foot on your palm and say "high five". Reward with treat and repeat as long as necessary.

Shake hands – Command your dog to sit then take his paw and say "shake hands". Give him a treat and say "good shake". Repeat until necessary.

Dance – Coton de Tulears commonly love to stand on their hind legs; they are gifted with good balance and body proportion so they can do it for long periods of time. Command him to sit down then hold a treat high above his head so that he'll have to stand on his hind legs. When he's standing on his hind legs, twirl the treat around so that he'll follow it and it will look like he's dancing. After a twirl, reward him with a treat and say "good dance". Repeat until he can do it on command.

Chapter Six: Training Your Coton de Tulear

Fetch– Coton de Tulears love to play fetch and it's a very good exercise for them. Plus, teaching your dog how to fetch is probably the most useful trick for him to learn. You'll get to teach him words, when you're lazy to get something he could get it for you, and it's an enjoyable game for him to play which serves as his daily exercise. You should start with items that will excite him like a ball, a chew toy or a bone. Make sure to properly and repeatedly label the item you are asking him to retrieve before throwing it and once he returns it, give him a reward. When his vocabulary expands, you can start making a game out of it by asking him to identify the item among a lot of other objects in the same place. Whenever he gets it right, it would be a good idea to increase the prize for motivation.

Chapter Six: Training Your Coton de Tulear

Chapter Seven: Grooming Your Coton de Tulear Properly

Grooming is the only high-maintenance aspect of owning a Coton de Tulear. Because of their long hair, frequent care is needed in order to maintain a healthy, tangle-free coat. If you neglect your grooming duties, you may end up needing to shave off your dog's hair. Fortunately, there is always the option of bringing your dog to a professional grooming service if you don't have the time or patience to do the task. This chapter is dedicated to teaching you how to groom your Coton de Tulear properly.

Chapter Seven: Grooming Your Coton de Tulear

Recommended Tools to Have on Hand

If you plan to groom your Coton de Tulear yourself you will need certain tools and supplies. Even if you choose to have your dog professionally groomed, you should still have some supplies available for daily brushing and occasional bathing. <u>You will find a list of several recommended grooming tools and supplies below</u>:

- Wire-pin brush
- Metal wide-tooth comb
- Slicker brush (or undercoat rake)
- Small, sharp scissors
- Dog-friendly shampoo
- Nail clippers
- Dog-friendly ear cleaning solution
- Dog toothbrush
- Dog-friendly toothpaste

Chapter Seven: Grooming Your Coton de Tulear

Recommended Brands for Grooming Supplies

Owners of Coton de Tulears voted on the top brands of shampoos, conditioners and brushes that they found most reliable and effective for grooming their dogs. **You will find these brands below:**

Shampoo

1 - Day to Day Moisturizing Shampoo by Chris Christensen. Gentle enough for everyday use, prevents matting, and keeps your dog's coat shiny.

2 - Isle of Dogs No. 10 Evening Primrose Oil Dog Shampoo Gentle enough for everyday use, keeps your dog's coat shiny, good for dogs with sensitive skin.

3 - Nature's Specialties Plum Silky Shampoo & Conditioner All in one concentrated shampoo and conditioner so it eliminates one step in bathing and a small amount will suffice. Good fragrance but not recommended for dogs who are sensitive to smell.

4 - MinkSheen 4 in 1 Pet Shampoo
Multipurpose product: shampoo, conditioner, anti-bacterial formula, and natural insect repellant.

Chapter Seven: Grooming Your Coton de Tulear

Conditioner

1 - BioGroom Silk Creme Rinse Conditioner for Dogs
Helps reduce static.

2 - Coat Handler Conditioner
Leave-in conditioner, helps reduce static, prevents mats and keeps the coat cleaner longer.

3 - Day to Day Moisturizing Conditioner by Chris
Reduces tangles.

4 - Isle of Dogs No. 51 Heavy Management Dog
Complements the Isle of Dogs shampoo.

Brushes

1 - Chris Christensen wood pin brushes

2 - Chris Christensen slicker brushes

3 - Chris Christensen Brat Buttercomb Long Tooth

4 - Les Poochs Matt Zapper

5 - Safari Dematting Comb

Chapter Seven: Grooming Your Coton de Tulear

Tips for Bathing and Grooming Coton de Tulear

Because Coton de Tulears have thick coats, you may want to have it cleaned and trimmed by a professional groomer. Even if you do, however, you will still need to brush your dog's coat on a daily basis to prevent mats and tangles. Brushing your Coton de Tulear's coat is very easy but it will take some time– just start at the base of the neck and work your way along the dog's back, down his legs, and under his belly. Always brush in the direction of hair growth and move slowly so you don't hurt your dog if you come across a snag.

If you encounter a mat or a tangle while brushing your Coton de Tulear, try using a wide-toothed comb to gently work through it. The more frequently you brush your Coton de Tulear, the less likely he is to develop mats and tangles. If you can't work the tangle out, you may need to cut it out of your dog's coat. Take a pair of sharp scissors in one hand and pinch the hair at the base of the mat (between the dog's skin and the mat) with your other hand – cut through the hairs a few at a time while gently pulling on the mat until it comes free.

Because of their long coats, Coton de Tulears tend to attract dirt and dust. If you need to bathe your Coton de Tulear you will want to brush him first. When you are ready

Chapter Seven: Grooming Your Coton de Tulear

for the bath, fill the bathtub with a few inches of warm (not hot) water and place your dog inside. Use a cup to pour water over your dog's back or use a handheld sprayer to wet down his coat. Once your dog's coat is dampened, apply a small amount of dog-friendly shampoo and work it into a lather. After shampooing, rinse your dog's coat thoroughly to get rid of all the soap and then towel him dry. If it is warm you might be able to let his coat air-dry but if it is cold you should finish it off with a blow dryer on the low heat setting.

While you might be able to handle brushing and bathing your Coton de Tulear yourself, trimming his coat is probably best left to the professionals. If you plan to show your dog you should go with the standard cut which does not actually involve any major trimming except for the fur on the feet to keep them neat – the groomer may also trim the fur on your dog's back to enhance his natural lines. If your Coton de Tulear is only being kept as a pet, you can feel free to keep his fur trimmed a little shorter – this will help to prevent mats and tangles, also keeping his coat smoother between brushings. If you want to trim your dog's coat yourself, ask the groomer to show you how to do it before you try it at home.

Chapter Seven: Grooming Your Coton de Tulear

Other Grooming Tasks

In addition to brushing and bathing your Coton de Tulear, you also need to engage in some other grooming tasks including trimming your dog's nails, cleaning his ears, cleaning his folds and wrinkles, caring for dry skin and nose, and brushing his teeth. <u>You will find an overview of each of these grooming tasks below</u>:

Trimming Your Dog's Nails

Your dog's nails grow in the same way that your own nails grow so they need to be trimmed occasionally. Before you trim your dog's nails for the first time you should have your veterinarian or a professional groomer show you how to do it. A dog's nail contains a quick – the blood vessel that supplies blood to the nail – and if you cut the nail too short you could sever it. A severed quick will cause your dog pain and it will bleed profusely. The best way to avoid cutting your dog's nails too short is to just trim the sharp tip.

Cleaning Your Dog's Ears

The Coton de Tulear has drop ears. If the dog's ears get wet it creates an environment that is beneficial for infection-causing bacteria. Regularly checking your dog's ears and

Chapter Seven: Grooming Your Coton de Tulear

making sure they are clean and dry is the key to preventing infections. If you have to clean your dog's ears, use a dog ear cleaning solution and squeeze a few drops into the ear canal. Then, massage the base of your dog's ears to distribute the solution then wipe it away using a clean cotton ball.

Brushing Your Dog's Teeth

Many dog owners neglect their dog's dental health which is a serious mistake. You should brush your dog's teeth with a dog-friendly toothbrush and dog toothpaste to preserve his dental health. Feeing your dog dental treats and giving him hard rubber toys can also help to maintain his dental health.

Chapter Eight: Breeding Coton de Tulears

Owing to the strictly enforced Code of Ethics of the Coton de Tulear Club of America, the breed has been preserved to be among the lucky ones that are not predisposed to genetic defects and illnesses. The Code of Ethics was established to protect this rare breed from irresponsible breeding and to ensure the maintenance of a healthy gene pool. In lieu of this, there aren't any specific details available to the public about breeding Coton de Tulears because the right to this information is reserved only for professional breeders (as it should be for all breeds because the lives of dogs deserve to be in good hands). Therefore, this chapter should be taken merely as an education on breeding dogs in general and not as an encouragement to breed your dogs in your backyard.

Chapter Eight: Breeding Coton de Tulears

Basic Dog Breeding Information

Before you decide whether or not to breed your Coton de Tulear, you should take the time to learn the basics about dog breeding in general.

The ASPCA recommends having your dogs neutered or spayed before the age of 6 months. For female dogs, six months is around the time the dog experiences her first heat. Heat is just another name for the estrus cycle in dogs and it generally lasts for about 14 to 21 days. The frequency of heat may vary slightly from one dog to another but it generally occurs twice a year. When your female dog goes into heat, this is when she is capable of becoming pregnant.

When breeding it is important that you wait until the female reaches sexual maturity. Your dog may be full-size by the time she reaches one year of age, but most breeders recommend waiting until she is two years old to breed her. Not only does this ensure that the dog is mature enough to physically carry and bear a litter, but it also provides enough time for any serious health problems to develop. If the dog does display signs of congenital health problems, she should not be bred for fear of passing them on. Preferably, your dog should only be bred every other year because if she conceives and gives birth consecutively within a short span of time it may cause problems in her reproductive system.

Chapter Eight: Breeding Coton de Tulears

Once you've made sure that you have chosen the ideal breeding pair you can start to think about the details of heat and breeding. When a female dog goes into heat there are a few common signs you can look for. The first sign of heat is swelling of the vulva – this may be accompanied by a bloody discharge. Over the course of the heat cycle the discharge lightens in color and becomes more watery. By the 10th day of the cycle the discharge is light pink – this is when she begins to ovulate and it is when she is most fertile. This is the time to introduce her to the male dog. If she isn't receptive to the male's advances, wait a day or two before trying again.

A dog is technically capable of conceiving at any point during the heat cycle because the male's sperm can survive in her reproductive tract for up to 5 days. If you don't plan to breed your dog, you need to keep her locked away while she is in heat. A male dog can smell a female dog in heat from several miles away and an intact male dog will go to great lengths to breed. Never take a female dog in heat to the dog park and be very careful about taking her outside at all. Do not leave her unattended in your backyard because a stray dog could get in and breed with her.

If you want to breed your dog, you will need to keep track of her estrus cycle so you know when to breed her. It generally takes a few years for a dog's cycle to become regular. Keep track of your dog's cycle on a calendar so you

Chapter Eight: Breeding Coton de Tulears

know when to breed her. Tracking her cycle and making note of when you introduce her to the male dog will help you predict the due date for the puppies. Once you do start breeding your dog, be sure to skip at least one heat cycle between litters – ideally, you should give your dog a year to rest between litters.

Breeding Tips and Raising Puppies

After the male dog fertilizes the egg inside the female's body, the female will go through the gestation period during which the puppies start to develop inside her womb. The gestation period for dogs usually lasts anywhere from 60 to 63 days with the average being 61. However, you won't be able to actually tell that your dog is pregnant until

Chapter Eight: Breeding Coton de Tulears

after the third week. By the 25th day of pregnancy it is safe for a vet to perform an ultrasound and by day 28 he should be able to feel the puppies by palpating the female's abdomen. At the six week mark an x-ray can be performed to check the size of the litter. The average litter size for Coton de Tulears is 5 puppies.

While the puppies are growing inside your female dog's belly you need to take careful care of her. You don't need to feed your dog any extra until the fourth or fifth week of pregnancy when she really starts to gain weight. Make sure to provide your dog with a healthy diet and keep up with regular vet appointments to make sure the pregnancy is progressing well. Once you reach the fifth week of pregnancy you can increase your dog's daily rations in proportion to her weight gain.

After eight weeks of gestation you should start to get ready for your dog to give birth – in dogs, this is called whelping. You should provide your dog with a clean, safe, and quiet place to give birth such as a large box in a dimly lit room. Line the box with old towels or newspapers for easy cleanup after the birth and make sure your dog has access to the box at all times. As she nears her due date she will start spending more and more time in the box.

When your dog is ready to give birth her internal temperature will decrease slightly. If you want to predict

Chapter Eight: Breeding Coton de Tulears

when the puppies will be born you can start taking her internal temperature once a day during the last week of gestation. When the dog's body temperature drops from 100°F to 102°F (37.7°C to 38.8°C to about 98°F (36.6°C), labor is likely to begin very soon. At this point your dog will display obvious signs of discomfort such as pacing, panting, or changing positions. Just let her do her own thing but keep an eye on her in case of complications.

During the early stages of labor, your dog will experience contractions about 10 minutes apart. If she has contractions for more than 2 hours without giving birth, bring her to the vet immediately. Once your dog starts whelping, she will whelp one puppy about every thirty minutes. After every puppy is born, she will clean it with her tongue – this will also help stimulate the puppy to start breathing on its own. After all of the puppies have been born, the mother will expel the afterbirth and the puppies will begin nursing.

It is essential that the puppies start nursing as soon as possible after whelping so that they get the colostrum. The colostrum is the first milk a mother produces and it is loaded with nutrients as well as antibodies that will protect the puppies while their own immune systems continue developing. The puppies will generally start nursing on their own or the mother will encourage them. After the puppies

Chapter Eight: Breeding Coton de Tulears

nurse for a little while you should make sure that your mother dog eats something as well.

The newborn Coton de Tulear puppies only weigh about 160-200 grams and they will continue growing over the next several months until they zone in on their adult size. It is a good idea to weigh the puppies once a week or so to make sure they are growing at a healthy rate. When puppies are born they will have some very fine hair but it isn't enough to keep them warm – your mother dog will help with that. It is also very important to place the puppies in a warm place or under a light.

Your puppies will be heavily dependent on their mother for the first few weeks of life until they start becoming more mobile. Around 5 to 6 weeks of age you should start offering your puppies small amounts of solid food soaked in broth or water to start the weaning process. Over the next few weeks the puppies will start to nurse less and eat more solid food. Around 8 weeks of age they should be completely weaned – this is when they are ready to be separated from their mother.

Chapter Eight: Breeding Coton de Tulears

Chapter Nine: Showing Your Coton de Tulear

Coton de Tulears love the limelight. They love competition and entertaining an audience with their tricks and skills. It's as if this breed was made to perform and participate in dog shows. So if you're interested in the idea of joining a dog show for the prestige and bonding experience with your dog, the first step is to find out if your Coton de Tulear is qualified as per the AKC breed standard. This chapter provides a summary of the standards of the AKC for a Coton de Tulear and how to prepare your dog for a show.

Chapter Nine: Showing Your Coton de Tulear

Coton de Tulear Breed Standard

The AKC breed standard for the Coton de Tulear provides guidelines for both breeding and showing. AKC-registered breeders must select dogs that adhere to the standards of the breed and all Coton de Tulear owners who seek to show their dogs at AKC shows must compare them to the official breed standard as well. <u>Below you will find an overview of the breed standard for the Coton de Tulear breed</u>:

General Appearance and Temperament

The Coton de Tulear's unique characteristic is its white cotton-like coat. It is a small but tough dog. The breed has bright and intelligent eyes with an animated smile. The main trait of the Coton de Tulear is its temperament: adaptable, steady, joyful, energetic and sociable.

Head and Neck

The head is short and triangular from the top view. The skull is somewhat rounded from the front view. It is wider than it is long. Round, black or brown eyes, set wide apart, with leveled corners and black pigmented eyelid rims. Droopy, triangular ears, set high on the head above the line of the

Chapter Nine: Showing Your Coton de Tulear

eyes, carried close to the cheeks and reaches up to the corners of the lips. Hair on ears can be white, tan, or black mixed with white that looks like gray. Straight, wide and big muzzle with a strong chin. Black, rounded triangle nose with open nostrils as an extension of the nasal line. Black, fine lips and tight flews. Scissor bite with aligned, white teeth. Neck is proportional to dog's length and height and connects smoothly to shoulders. It is medium in length and slightly arched.

Body and Tail

The body is longer than it is tall. The height is two-thirds of the length giving the impression of a rectangular shape. The chest is long, well-pronounced and well-let down to elbow level, protruding forward of the point of shoulder. The ribs are well-sprung. The belly is tucked-up. The back is strong. The loin is well-muscled and short. The croup is oblique, short and muscled. The tail is low set in extension of the spinal column. It is curved over the back.

Legs and Feet

The front legs are upright, vertical and parallel. They are well-muscled with good bone. The hind legs are muscular from hip to hock. The feet are small and round with tight and arched toes. The pads are completely pigmented black. Dewclaws may be left natural or may be removed.

Coat and Texture

The coat has the texture of cotton. It is very soft and sinuous. The coat is thick, bounteous and can be very slightly wavy.

Color

Preferably pure white but light tan or gray is acceptable in the ears. Light tan shadings are acceptable on five percent of the body. Puppies that are less than a year old are permitted to have light tan, light brown, dark brown, chestnut or grey on the body and head as they are expected to fade eventually.

Size

Female dogs should be 9 – 10 inches high and should weigh between 8 – 13 pounds. Male dogs should be 10 – 11 inches high and should weigh between 9 – 15 pounds.

Gait

The gait should be steady, free and easy.

Chapter Nine: Showing Your Coton de Tulear

Disqualifications

- Eyes other than black or brown
- No tail
- Color black on the body
- Lack of pigment on nose, eye rims, and lips
- Female dog shorter than 8 ½ inches or higher than 11 inches
- Male dog shorter than 9 ½ inches or higher than 12 inches
- Looped tail
- Tail that doesn't reach the hock
- Tail that is carried flat over the body
- Any color except 5 percent of light tan on coat
- Bulging large eye/s
- Almond-shaped eyes
- Wheel or flat back
- Wooly, silky or curly hair

Chapter Nine: Showing Your Coton de Tulear

Preparing Your Coton de Tulear for Show

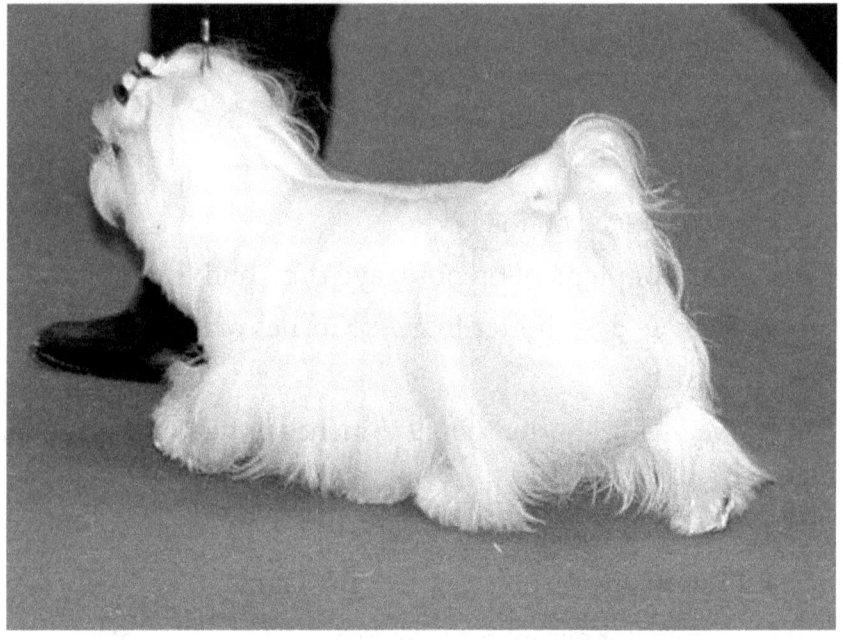

Once you've determined that your Coton de Tulear is a good representation of the official breed standard, then you can think about entering him in a dog show. Dog shows occur all year-round in many different locations so check the AKC or Kennel Club website for shows in your area. Remember, the rules for each show will be different so make sure to do your research so that you and your dog are properly prepared for the show.

On the following page you will find a list of some general and specific recommendations to follow during show prep:

Chapter Nine: Showing Your Coton de Tulear

- Make sure that your dog is properly socialized to be in an environment with many other dogs and people.

- Ensure that your dog is completely housetrained and able to hold his bladder for at least several hours.

- Solidify your dog's grasp of basic obedience – he should listen and follow basic commands.

- Do some research to learn the requirements for specific shows before you choose one – make sure your dog meets all the requirements for registration.

- Make sure that your dog is caught up on his vaccinations (especially Bordetella since he will be around other dogs) and have your vet clear his overall health for show.

- Have your dog groomed about a week before the show and then take the necessary steps to keep his coat clean and in good condition.

Chapter Nine: Showing Your Coton de Tulear

In addition to making sure that your dog meets the requirements for the show and is a good representation of the AKC breed standard, you should also pack a bag of supplies that you will need on the day of show. <u>Below you will find a list of helpful things to include in your dog show supply pack</u>:

- Registration information
- Dog crate or exercise pen
- Grooming table and grooming supplies
- Food and treats
- Food and water bowls
- Trash bags
- Medication (if needed)
- Change of clothes
- Food/water for self
- Paper towels or rags
- Toys for the dog

If you want to show your dog but you don't want to jump immediately into an AKC show, you may be able to find some local dog shows in your area. Local shows may be put on by a branch of a national Coton de Tulear breed club and they can be a great place to learn and to connect with other Coton de Tulear owners.

Chapter Ten: Keeping Your Dog Healthy

Coton de Tulears earn a hundred points for keeping them as pets just because they are one of the lucky breeds that are generally very healthy and aren't commonly afflicted by health problems. They aren't affected by a particular disorder or disease that is specific to their breed. The entire gene pool of the Coton de Tulear is relatively healthy and free from genetic anomalies. In this chapter, you will learn about some of the most common conditions that affect all dog breeds in general and though they aren't widespread, have been seen in Coton de Tulears.

Chapter Ten: Keeping Your Dog Healthy

Common Health Problems Affecting Coton de Tulears

It is quite a mysterious miracle that the Coton de Tulear is a healthy breed because it was revived from extinction by inbreeding which would normally cause an increase in genetic abnormalities. This rare breed has a small gene pool which should make the occurrence of diseases more likely. But of course, it is a welcome phenomenon to have the world blessed with a very lovable breed that can live a long and healthy life.

In this section you will receive an overview of some of the conditions occasionally seen in Coton de Tulears. By educating yourself about the cause, presentation, and treatment for these common conditions you can help to keep your Coton de Tulear in good health for as long as possible. Some of the common conditions affecting Coton de Tulear dogs include:

- Hip dyplasia
- Patellar Luxation
- Progressive Retinal Atrophy

Chapter Ten: Keeping Your Dog Healthy

Hip Dysplasia

Hip dysplasia is a very common musculoskeletal problem among dogs. In a normal hip, the head of the femur (thigh bone) sits snugly within the groove of the hip joint and it rotates freely within the grove as the dog moves. Hip dysplasia occurs when the femoral head becomes separated from the hip joint – this is called subluxation. This could occur as a result of abnormal joint structure or laxity in the muscles and ligaments supporting the joint.

This condition can present in puppies as young as 5 months of age or in older dogs. The most common symptoms of hip dysplasia include pain or discomfort, limping, hopping, or unwillingness to move. As the condition progresses, the dog's pain will increase and he may develop osteoarthritis. The dog may begin to lose muscle tone and might even become completely lame in the affected joint.

Genetics are the largest risk factor for hip dysplasia, though nutrition and exercise are factors as well. Diagnosis for hip dysplasia is made through a combination of clinical signs, physical exam, and x-rays. Surgical treatments for hip dysplasia are very common and generally highly effective. Medical treatments may also be helpful to reduce osteoarthritis and to manage pain.

Chapter Ten: Keeping Your Dog Healthy

Patellar Luxation

Patellar luxation is a musculoskeletal condition in which the patella (or kneecap) slides out of its normal anatomic position within the groove of the femur (thigh bone). This condition is one of the most common joint abnormalities in dogs and it is particularly common in small and toy breeds like the Maltese, Pomeranian, Yorkshire Terrier and the Boston Terrier. It is also more common in female dogs than in male dogs.

In the early stages of the condition, many dogs do not display serious symptoms. They might experience some soreness or tenderness after the patella pops back into place but they may still be able to walk normally. The more frequently the dislocation occurs, however, the more wear and tear on the bone and joint the dog will suffer. This leads to osteoarthritis and pain, potentially even lameness in the joint. The dog generally doesn't experience pain while the kneecap is dislocated, but he will when it pops back into its rightful place.

The cause of patellar luxation is usually the result of a genetic malformation or some kind of trauma. Unfortunately, medical treatments are rarely effective and surgery is usually required to achieve long-term relief. After surgery the dog will need to limit its mobility and regular vet check-ups are recommended.

Chapter Ten: Keeping Your Dog Healthy

Progressive Retinal Atrophy

This is a degenerative disease that affects the retina of the eye – the part of the eye that is sensitive to light. PRA generally occurs in both eyes at the same time and it may lead to total blindness, though it is not painful for the dog. In fact, many dogs adapt well to a loss of vision as long as furniture and objects are kept in the same location around the home.

There are several forms of PRA characterized by the age of onset and the rate of progression. In most dogs, the photoreceptors in the retina of the eye develop around 8 weeks of age. If the dog has PRA, the retinas might not develop as well or they could begin degenerating at this point. Dogs with PRA generally experience degeneration within two months of birth and most of them go completely blind within a year.

Though PRA is not painful for your dog, it does affect his ability to see. The outward appearance of the eye is generally normal (no tearing or inflammation) but you might notice signs of changing vision. For example, the dog might have trouble seeing at night or it might be reluctant to go down stairs. Eventually the pupil will become dilated and, in some cases, the lens becomes cloudy or opaque.

Chapter Ten: Keeping Your Dog Healthy

Preventing Illness with Vaccinations

The best way to keep your dog healthy is to provide him with a nutritious and balanced diet. You also need to ensure that he gets proper veterinary care, and that includes routine vaccinations. Vaccinations will not protect your dog against nutritional deficiencies or inherited conditions, but they can help to protect him from certain communicable diseases like rabies, distemper, and parvovirus.

The vaccinations your dog needs may vary depending where you live since certain regions have a higher risk for certain diseases. Your vet will know which vaccinations your dog needs and when he needs them, but the vaccination schedule below will help you to keep track of when your dog needs to see the vet.

To give you an idea what kind of vaccinations your puppy will need, consult the vaccination schedule below:

Vaccination Schedule for Dogs**			
Vaccine	**Doses**	**Age**	**Booster**
Rabies	1	12 weeks	annual
Distemper	3	6-16 weeks	3 years
Parvovirus	3	6-16 weeks	3 years
Adenovirus	3	6-16 weeks	3 years
Parainfluenza	3	6 weeks, 12-	3 years

Chapter Ten: Keeping Your Dog Healthy

		14 weeks	
Bordetella	1	6 weeks	annual
Lyme Disease	2	9, 13-14 weeks	annual
Leptospirosis	2	12 and 16 weeks	annual
Canine Influenza	2	6-8, 8-12 weeks	annual

** Keep in mind that vaccine requirements may vary from one region to another. Only your vet will be able to tell you which vaccines are most important for the region where you live.

Chapter Ten: Keeping Your Dog Healthy

Coton de Tulear Care Sheet

In reading this book, you have received a combination of valuable facts, instructions and advice that has given you a comprehensive understanding of caring for a Coton de Tulear as a pet. If you have decided to get your own Coton de Tulear, you will still find this book useful as you spend your days living with your dog. But rather than flipping through the entire book, you can use this care sheet as your quick reference for the most basic information you might want to recall and review. This care sheet is a summary of all the useful things that a Coton de Tulear owner needs.

Coton de Tulear Care Sheet

1.) Basic Coton de Tulear Information

Pedigree: Madagascar

AKC Group: Companion, Non-sporting

Breed Size: small and sturdy

Height: female dogs – 9 to 10 inches, male dogs – 10 to 11 inches

Weight: female dogs – 8 to 13 pounds, male dogs – 9 to 15 pounds

Coat Length: long

Coat Texture: cotton-like

Shedding: none

Color: white, occasional light tan or gray in ears

Eyes: brown or black

Nose: black

Ears: droopy

Tail: curved over the back

Temperament: affectionate, playful, adaptable, sociable, intelligent, easygoing

Strangers: generally friendly to everyone

Children: generally good with children, but (like all dogs) should be supervised around young and small children

Other Dogs: generally good with other dogs and other animals if properly trained and socialized

Training: very easy

Exercise Needs: minimal exercise needed – daily walks, outdoor and indoor physical activities would be sufficient

Health Conditions: ordinarily no known health issues

Lifespan: 14 – 19 years

2.) Habitat Requirements

Recommended Accessories: crate, dog bed, fences/gates, food/water dishes, toys, leash, collar, grooming supplies

Collar: sized by weight

Grooming Supplies: shampoo and conditioner for dogs, wire-pin brush, metal wide-tooth comb, slicker brush (or undercoat rake)

Grooming Frequency: brush daily and bathe weekly

Energy Level: high – ranges from being playful to boisterous

Exercise Requirements: daily, around 30 minutes

Crate: required

Crate Size: just large enough for dog to lie down and turn around comfortably

Crate Extras: bed

Toys: partial to squeaky toys

Exercise Ideas: walks or indoor/outdoor games

Food/Water bowls: stainless steel or ceramic bowls, clean daily

3.) Nutritional Needs

Nutritional Needs: water, protein, carbohydrate, fats, vitamins, minerals

Restrictions: grains, soy, corn

Calorie Needs: varies by age, weight, and activity level

Amount to Feed (puppy): ¾ cup a day

Amount to Feed (adult): ¾ cup a day

Feeding Frequency: two to four meals daily

Important Ingredients: fresh animal protein (chicken, beef, lamb, turkey, eggs), digestible carbohydrates, animal fats

Important Minerals: calcium, phosphorus, potassium, magnesium, iron, copper and manganese

Important Vitamins: Vitamin A, Vitamin A, Vitamin B-12, Vitamin D, Vitamin C

Look For: AAFCO statement of nutritional adequacy; protein at top of ingredients list; no artificial flavors, dyes, preservatives

4.) Breeding Information

Age of First Heat: around 6 months (or earlier)

Heat (Estrus) Cycle: 14 to 21 days

Frequency: twice a year, every 6 to 7 months

Greatest Fertility: 11 to 15 days into the cycle

Gestation Period: average 63 days

Pregnancy Detection: possible after 21 days, best to wait 28 days before exam

Feeding Pregnant Dogs: maintain normal diet until week 5 or 6 then slightly increase rations

Signs of Labor: body temperature drops below normal 100° to 102°F (37.7° to 38.8°C), may be as low as 98°F (36.6°C); dog begins nesting in a dark, quiet place

Contractions: period of 10 minutes in waves of 3 to 5 followed by a period of rest

Whelping: puppies are born in 1/2 hour increments following 10 to 30 minutes of forceful straining

Puppies: born with eyes and ears closed; eyes open at 3 weeks, teeth develop at 10 weeks

Litter Size: average 5 puppies

Size at Birth: 160-200 grams

Weaning: start offering puppy food soaked in water at 6 weeks; fully weaned by 8 weeks

Socialization: start as early as possible to prevent puppies from being nervous as an adult

5.) *First Aid Kit*

In case of an emergency, all dog owners should have a first aid kit which consists of the following:

- Magnifying glass
- Scissors
- Tweezers
- Nail clippers and metal nail file

Coton de Tulear Care Sheet

- Styptic powder
- Penlight
- Eye dropper or oral syringe
- Cotton swabs
- Cotton balls
- Clean towels – cloth and paper
- Rectal thermometer
- Lubricant such as mineral oil or Petroleum Jelly
- Disposable gloves
- Bitter Apple or other product to discourage chewing
- Pet carrier
- 2 Towels or blankets to use as a stretcher and insulator
- Cold packs and heat packs (wrap in towel before using)
- Wound disinfectant such as Betadine or Nolvasan
- Triple antibiotic ointment for skin
- Antibiotic ophthalmic ointment for eyes, e.g., Terramycin
- Eye wash solution
- Sterile saline
- Antidiarrheal medicine
- Antihistamine for allergic reactions
- Cortisone spray to aid in itch relief
- Ear cleaning solution
- Hydrogen peroxide
- Activated charcoal to absorb ingested poisons
- Square gauze of various sizes – some sterile
- Non-stick pads
- First aid tape – both paper and adhesive types
- Bandage rolls – gauze and Vetwrap
- Band-Aids

Important Note: Before administering first aid on your dog, be sure to consult your veterinarian and ask about the important data you need.

Index

A

accessories 10, 14, 95
active 28, 30, 38
Adenovirus 91
adopt 11, 19, 22, 23, 24
adult 11, 22, 23, 51, 76, 96, 98
age 4, 13, 51, 71, 77, 88, 90, 91, 96, 97
AKC 4, 11, 21, 78, 79, 83, 85, 94
allergies 18, 46
antibodies 76
appearance 17, 79, 90

B

bark 3, 18, 36
bathing 62, 63, 65, 66, 67
bed 11, 12, 14, 40, 95, 96beh
behavior 3, 39, 53, 54, 56
blood 67, 72
body 31, 43, 44, 59, 74, 75, 80, 81, 82, 97
Bordetella 84, 92
bowls 10, 12, 14, 38, 39, 40, 85, 96
breed standard 31, 78, 79, 83, 85
breeder 11, 13, 19, 20, 21, 22, 23, 25, 26, 27, 28, 29, 31, 70, 71, 79
breeding 20, 25, 26, 27, 28, 70, 71, 72, 73, 74, 79, 87, 97
brush 15, 39. 62, 63, 64, 65, 68, 95

C

Canine Influenza 92
carbohydrates 43, 44, 46, 96

Coton de Tulears as Pets

care 16, 22, 23, 35, 36, 55, 61, 75, 91, 93
care sheet 93
cause 3, 47, 67, 71, 87, 89
chewing 12, 39, 99
children 5, 51, 95
clinic 13, 88
clipping 10
coat 2, 4, 15, 31, 46, 61, 62, 63, 64, 65, 66, 79, 81, 82, 84, 94
collar 13, 14, 16, 38, 39, 52, 95
color 4, 31, 46, 51, 72, 81, 82, 94
colostrum 76
command 54, 55, 57, 58, 59, 84
companion 2, 4, 9, 18, 37, 38, 94
condition 5, 20, 28, 46, 47, 84, 86, 87, 88, 89, 91, 95
crate 10, 11, 12, 14, 36, 40, 41, 56, 57, 85, 95, 96

D

diarrhea 30
diet 15, 42, 43, 44, 75, 91, 97
discharge 31, 72
discoloration 31
disease 9, 86, 87, 90, 91, 92
disorder 86
dog food 15, 42, 44, 45, 46, 47
dog license 8

E

ears 4, 31, 67, 68, 79, 80, 81, 94, 98
eating 32, 47
estrus cycle 71, 72
exercise 5, 18, 35, 37, 60, 85, 88, 95, 96
eyes 3, 4, 31, 56, 79, 80, 82, 90, 94, 98, 99

F

family	29, 37
fats	46, 96
fertile	72
food allergies	46

G

games	37, 58, 96
genetic	70, 86, 87, 88, 89
gestation period	74, 97
grooming	2, 3, 10, 14, 15, 16, 17, 36, 38, 39, 61, 62, 63, 65, 67, 85, 95

H

habitat	35, 37, 95
hair	31, 61, 65, 77, 80, 82
harness	39
health problems	71, 86, 87
height	2, 4, 80, 94
history	1, 6, 25

I

illness	31, 70, 91
ingredients	45, 46, 96, 97
inherited	91
initial costs	10, 14

K

kennel	21
Kennel Club	3, 21, 83

L

labor	75, 76, 97
leash	14, 38, 39, 52, 95
lethargic	30
lifespan	3, 5, 95
litter	20, 22, 30, 40, 57, 71, 73, 74, 98
litter size	74, 98

M

microchipping	10, 12, 14
minerals	43, 44, 96, 97
money	11, 13
monthly costs	10, 15, 16, 17
muzzle	80

N

nails	67
neuter	10, 13, 14, 23, 71
nursing	76
nutrients	76
nutritional needs	42, 43, 44, 45, 96

P

Parainfluenza	91
parents	26, 27
Parvovirus	91
personality	2, 17, 23, 29, 56, 57
Pet Poison Control	48
play	12, 30, 38, 58, 60
positive reinforcement	53, 54, 57, 58

pregnant	71, 74, 97
pros and cons	17
puppy mill	20, 21
puppy playpen	40
puppy-proofing	19, 32
purebred	11

R

rabies	8, 91
registration	21, 25, 84, 85
requirements	12, 35, 36, 37, 84, 85, 92, 95
rescue	11, 22, 23, 24

S

safety	38
shampoo	64, 65, 67, 99
shelter	13, 22
show	59, 66, 67, 78, 79, 83, 84, 85
signs	31, 71, 72, 75, 88, 90, 98
skin	13, 18, 46, 51, 53, 60, 63, 65, 67, 99
socialization	9, 27, 51, 98
spay	10, 13, 14, 23, 71
supplies	10, 14, 38, 39, 62, 63, 67, 85, 95
surgery	10, 13, 23, 89
swollen	31
symptoms	88, 89

T

tail	4, 80, 82
teeth	67, 68, 80, 98
temperament	2, 4, 79, 94
temperature	75, 98

tips 29, 42, 65, 74
toxic 33, 48
toys 10, 11, 12, 14, 16, 33, 38, 39, 40, 41, 68, 85, 95, 96
training 5, 26, 27, 37, 39, 41, 50, 53, 54, 55, 56, 57, 58, 95
treatment 87, 88, 89
treats 15, 17, 41, 68, 85
trim 66, 67

V

vaccinations 10, 13, 14, 28, 84, 91
veterinarian 16, 67, 100
vitamins 43, 44, 96, 97

W

water 10, 12, 14, 33, 38, 40, 44, 45, 52, 66, 72, 77, 85, 95, 96, 98
weight 2, 4, 43, 44, 46, 75, 94, 95, 96
whelping 75, 76, 98

References

"Coton de Tulear." Wikipedia.
<https://en.wikipedia.org/wiki/Coton_de_Tulear>

"Coton de Tulear Temperament - What's Good About 'Em, What's Bad About 'E." YourPureBredPuppy.
<http://www.yourpurebredpuppy.com/reviews/cotondetulear.html>

"Rescue & Adoption: Why Adult Coton de Tulears Make Better Pets." Adopt a Pet.
<http://www.adoptapet.com/s/adopt-a-coton-de-tulear>

"The Complete Coton de Tulear Guide." Coton de Tulear Care.
<http://www.coton-de-tulear-care.com/>

"Coton de Tulear." DogTime.
<http://dogtime.com/dog-breeds/coton-de-tulear">

"The Coton de Tulear!" The Dog Guide.
<http://www.dogguide.net/coton-de-tulear.php">

"Coton de Tulears." TerrificPets. <http://www.terrificpets.com/dog_breeds/coton_de_tulear.asp>

"Official Standard of the Coton de Tulear." AKC. <http://cdn.akc.org/CotondeTulear.pdf?_ga=1.69425936.1413678337.1464122831>

Photo Credits

Introduction Photo by Caronna via Wikimedia.

<https://commons.wikimedia.org/wiki/File:Coton_de_Tular_2.jpg>

Chapter 1 Photo by Willie Whitby via Wikimedia.

<https://commons.wikimedia.org/wiki/File:Coton_de_Tulear.jpg>

Breed History Photo by Poodle Girl via Wikimedia.

<https://commons.wikimedia.org/wiki/File:Maya_Bow.jpg>

Chapter 2 Photo by CamilleVila via Wikimedia.

<https://commons.wikimedia.org/wiki/File:Photos_188.JPG>

Chapter 3 Photo by CamilleVila via Wikimedia.

<https://commons.wikimedia.org/wiki/File:Photos_193.JPG>

Purchasing vs. Adopting a Rescue Photo by Cvf-ps via Wikimedia.

<https://commons.wikimedia.org/wiki/File:Emilio_Coton_de_Tulear.JPG>

Tips for Selecting a Healthy Coton de Tulear Puppy Photo by Slaunger via Wikimedia.

<https://commons.wikimedia.org/wiki/File:Coton_de_Tulear_Puppy-5899.jpg>

Chapter 4 Photo by fmxrider11 via Wikimedia.
<https://commons.wikimedia.org/wiki/File:FancyCoton.JPG>

Habitat and Exercise Requirements Photo by janbystrom via Wikimedia.
<https://commons.wikimedia.org/wiki/File:Cotondetulear.JPG>

Setting Up Your Puppy's Area Photo by Yukutsu via Wikimedia.
<https://commons.wikimedia.org/wiki/File:Coton_de_Tul%C3%A9ar2.jpg>

Chapter 5 Photo by BMarcell via Wikimedia.
<https://commons.wikimedia.org/wiki/File:A_Coton_de_Tul%C3%A9ar.jpg>

Chapter 6 Photo by Nefertury via Wikimedia.
<https://commons.wikimedia.org/wiki/File:LoloCoton.jpg>

Positive Reinforcement Photo by Caronna via Wikimedia.
<https://commons.wikimedia.org/wiki/File:Coton_de_Tular_1.jpg>

Chapter 7 Photo by Nicole via Wikimedia.
<https://commons.wikimedia.org/wiki/File:Coton_De_Tulear.jpg>

Chapter 8 Photo by Nefertury via Wikimedia.
<https://commons.wikimedia.org/wiki/File:Cotondetulearbaby.JPG>

Breeding Tips and Raising Puppies Photo by Maybo975 via Wikimedia.
<https://commons.wikimedia.org/wiki/File:Coton_de_Tulear_puppy.jpg>

Chapter 9 Photo by Pets Adviser via Wikimedia.
<https://commons.wikimedia.org/wiki/File:Coton_de_Tulear_-_Ch_Mi-Toi%27s_Burberry_At_Justincredible_aka_Burberry_3_(16415441310).jpg>

Preparing your Coton de Tulear for Show Photo by Jurriaan Schulman via Wikimedia.
<https://commons.wikimedia.org/wiki/File:Coton-De-Tulear.jpg>

Chapter 10 Photo by Jean via Wikimedia.
<https://commons.wikimedia.org/wiki/File:Coton_de_Tulear_dog.jpg>

Care Sheet Photo by Saffana via Wikimedia.
<https://commons.wikimedia.org/wiki/File:Baby_Hope_Guinness_Book.JPG>

Feeding Baby
Cynthia Cherry
978-1941070000

Axolotl
Lolly Brown
978-0989658430

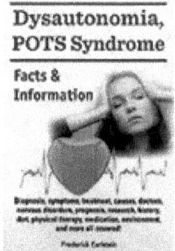

Dysautonomia, POTS Syndrome
Frederick Earlstein
978-0989658485

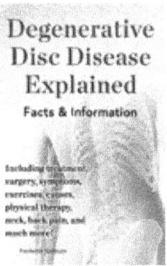

Degenerative Disc Disease Explained
Frederick Earlstein
978-0989658485

Sinusitis, Hay Fever,
Allergic Rhinitis Explained
Frederick Earlstein
978-1941070024

Wicca
Riley Star
978-1941070130

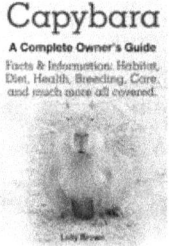

Zombie Apocalypse
Rex Cutty
978-1941070154

Capybara
Lolly Brown
978-1941070062

Eels As Pets
Lolly Brown
978-1941070167

Scabies and Lice Explained
Frederick Earlstein
978-1941070017

Saltwater Fish As Pets
Lolly Brown
978-0989658461

Torticollis Explained
Frederick Earlstein
978-1941070055

Kennel Cough
Lolly Brown
978-0989658409

Physiotherapist, Physical Therapist
Christopher Wright
978-0989658492

Rats, Mice, and Dormice As Pets
Lolly Brown
978-1941070079

Wallaby and Wallaroo Care
Lolly Brown
978-1941070031

Bodybuilding Supplements
Explained
Jon Shelton
978-1941070239

Demonology
Riley Star
978-19401070314

Pigeon Racing
Lolly Brown
978-1941070307

Dwarf Hamster
Lolly Brown
978-1941070390

Cryptozoology
Rex Cutty
978-1941070406

Eye Strain
Frederick Earlstein
978-1941070369

Inez The Miniature Elephant
Asher Ray
978-1941070353

Vampire Apocalypse
Rex Cutty
978-1941070321

www.ingramcontent.com/pod-product-compliance
Lightning Source LLC
Chambersburg PA
CBHW071706040426
42446CB00011B/1934